INTRODUC⌐

It was the Duke of York, later King Georg
speech to the Royal Academy in 1924 that the old custom of identifying
villages with carved or painted name signs ought to be revived. By
then, the Kent village of Biddenden had already won a Daily Mail
Competition in 1920 for its sign featuring the two Biddenden Maids on
what remains probably the best-known of all the county's village signs.
Several villages celebrated the Coronation of Queen Elizabeth II in
1953 with specially designed signs and more followed.

Although Kent lagged behind some other counties, it has caught up
rapidly in recent years and an outbreak of 'Millennium' signs has meant
that about half of all the county's villages are now identified with
attractive signs of their own. Some of the earlier ones have been
replaced by new ones; some have been removed completely; and
several more villages have plans to install a sign in the near future.

This selection of some of the most distinctive and interesting village
signs in Kent brings the county into line with other counties that have
already had selections of their village signs published and it includes
many that were illustrated in the weekly series published by the Kent
Messenger in 2001/2 by staff photographers. They all have something
to say about the villages they represent, many of which, because of
Kent's pre-eminent role in British history, are heirs to some of the
country's most colourful relics of history and legend.

Alan Bignell 2004.

KEMSING

The West Kent village of Kemsing, just north-east of Sevenoaks, centres upon St Edith's Well, which is the single feature on the village sign, where St Edith herself kneels beside it.

The well is surrounded by a walled garden behind the village war memorial and it feeds a small stream. A tablet on the wall relates that the well is within the precincts of the convent where St Edith (961-984), daughter of King Edgar, grew up. It is said that the water was hallowed by her presence and became a source of healing.

Although Edith was born in Kemsing, she lived most of her life in Wilton Abbey in Wiltshire. She was only 24 when she died but by then she had already become known as a miracle worker and the shrine which was built in her memory at Kemsing prospered for many years from the generosity of visiting pilgrims.

The saint is also commemorated with a statue, surmounted by a clock and a bell, on the front of St Edith's Village Hall, which was given to the village in 1911.

Every 10 years, since 1961 when the village celebrated the 1,000th anniversary of St Edith's birth, a festival has been held on her feast day, September 16th and the church (St Mary the Virgin) treasures the Kemsing Embroidery which was worked by 44 villagers and depicts village features in a series of roundels on a linen ground.

KINGSWOOD

Most of Kingswood is relatively new, built up in the second half of the 20th century, although some hints of its greater antiquity still exist.

Its village sign has identified Kingswood to travellers turning on to the Sutton Valence road for very much longer than neighbouring Broomfield has advertised itself with its village sign, but the two communities are linked by being part of the parish of Broomfield and Kingswood and both have centuries old links with nearby Leeds Castle.

Kingswood takes its name from the woodlands which were owned by the King, certainly in the 15th century and probably from soon after Edward I's Queen Eleanor of Castile became the owner of Leeds Castle during the 13th century. The Royal ownership is reflected in the village sign which, within its simple boxed wooden frame, depicts a crown above the name of the village, beneath which is a design of trees. Surmounting the frame is the Kent White Horse badge. The heraldic pun of the illustration is simple and direct and it says pretty well all there is to say about Kingswood.

The sign stands just off the road to East Sutton, on a piece of land adjoining and belonging to the village hall. It was commissioned by Broomfield and Kingswood parish council and made by the Coxheath-based craftsman Bernard Hill, who has been responsible for making many of Kent's village signs, employing a technique that uses resin casting.

LADDINGFORD

There is more to the village sign at Laddingford than meets the eye. What does meet the eye is a rather colourful scene showing the River Tiese flowing under the 14th century stone bridge on its way to join the Medway at Yalding. The scene is bordered with trees and blossom and has the name of the village across the bottom and it hangs in a metal frame topped with decorative wrought ironwork and supported on scrolled iron brackets.

The sign stands on a grassy roadside bank, and the metal plate on the supporting upright successfully avoids meeting the eye of virtually anyone who might want to read that: "Within this post is a time capsule prepared by the children of Laddingford C of E Primary School, 1995."

The notice is so high up on the post that only an exceptionally tall reader is addressed by its plea: "Please take care of me until 2088 when I will gladly reveal my secrets."

(If the quoted dates are not entirely accurate, blame the height of the notice and the effect of weather on the lettering.)

There is not a great deal to Laddingford, yet it earned international prominence in 1997 when a local farmer exhibited at the annual Marden Fruit Show an apple weighing 3lb 11oz. That was big enough to earn it a place in the Guinness Book of Records as the world's largest apple, and the notice of a large part of the world's press.

A bronze cast was made of the apple so that an incredulous posterity should never be able to forget the fleeting, fruity fame of little Laddingford.

LAMBERHURST

This sign stands beside the A21, the main road through Lamberhurst, before it crosses the River Tiese lower down. It is a rather pretty oval of painted decorative ironwork with painted symbols that include the White Horse of Kent, an oast house and, of course, a lamb.

Once, the Kent-Sussex border ran through the village but when the two counties decided it would be administratively tidier if it were in one or the other, local people voted to pay their dues in Kent because the hops they grew fetched a higher price there.

Before hops, it was iron that drove the local economy and Lamberhurst forge was one of the most famous of the Wealden ironworks, supplying, among much more, railings for St Paul's Cathedral, an example of which came back to the village in 1976 and is now to be seen in the main street beside the village hall. Today, Lamberhurst vineyard is a major contributor to Kent's wine-growing industry.

The surrounding area is rich in old buildings, including the landmark Scotney Castle, and nearby Bewl Water reservoir, the first sod for which was lifted in 1973, today attracts thousands of anglers, water sports enthusiasts, wildlife watchers and walkers as well as ensuring the water supply for much of the county.

St Mary's church, a little distance outside the village, is worth a visit for the view from the car park, where the yew tree is known to have stood for 1,500 years.

LANGLEY

Langley is one of those villages that seldom get so much as a mention in county guide books, suggesting that, on the whole, history has not tended to linger there very long.

Nevertheless, it has had a village sign, erected by the parish council, longer than many more high-profile villages. It is painted on shield-shaped metal, separated horizontally into three parts. The top part bears the village name in bold black lettering across the White Horse on a red ground. Below that is a symbolic illustration of the village, with trees and oasts, water representing the Langley locks, and St Mary's church, all on a white ground. The triangular lower third bears a ring of friendship with the French fleur-de-lys and the English rose on a blue ground, recalling the twinship with the French community of Bray-sur-Somme.

The name of the village is said to derive from an old English description of a long clearing and it featured in written records in the 9th century. William I's Domesday bureaucrats in 1085 or thereabouts, recorded that it comprised a church, land for four ploughs, including three acres of meadow and enough woodland to sustain 25 pigs. It was peopled by seven villagers with five smallholders and seven slaves and they assessed the value at 60 shillings (£3).

The parish council made sure that future villagers would have some history to boast of when they buried a lead-lined steel casket beneath the playing field, intending it to be brought to light in 2400 AD to reveal photographs, copies of the parish magazine and other mementos of village life in 1979.

LEIGH

The sign that was erected on the edge of the large village green in 1951 is a rectangular iron framework around a colourful quartered shield with the name of the village and the date on a metal ribbon over the top. The quarterings on the shield illustrate, at the top, a deer (representing the former Leigh Place deer park), and an old stone bridge, and below them is a lychgate and a cricketer in play on the village green.

Hall Place, once Leigh Hall, was built in 1876 for the Nottinghamshire merchant and philanthropist Samuel Morley, MP and the red-brick building in its 200 acres of gardens and parkland, as well as the imposing gateway, were designed by the Victorian architect George Devey. The house was severely damaged by fire in 1976 and close-by St Mary's Church, too, owes something of its present appearance to a fire which caused damage to it in the 15th century.

Whatever similarly named villages elsewhere in the country call themselves, this one is pronounced Lie (as in untruth), and it is said to signify a sheltered place, which this undeniably is. The village green was owned by the lord of the manor, Lord Hollenden, until he handed it over to the parish council in January 1948.

LENHAM

The village sign that stands at the point where the road into Lenham forks off the A20 has been there since 1993 and is unusual in that it is unframed other than by the foliage that forms part of the domed illustration itself.

It is a fairly colourful, sculpted sign featuring the church, local old buildings and the hillside cross that was created by exposing the chalk in 1922 as a village memorial to 42 local casualties of the First World War and now commemorates further victims of World War Two.

The springs that bubble forth at Lenham are the source of the little River Len which flows in a roughly north-westerly course to join the River Medway at Maidstone, pausing along the way to provide Leeds Castle with its moat. Once, it powered at least 25, and probably more, water mills, some of which earned mention in the 11th century Domesday Survey.

The spring water was ideal for growing watercress, too, which became a notable local product and Lenham was once renowned for the quality of its watercress - and also, oddly enough, for the quarrelsome nature of its women!

Mediaeval Lenham was a sufficiently important trading centre to be granted a market charter by Henry III in the 13th century but the most celebrated inhabitant of the parish was Mary Honywood, wife of Robert Honywood of Charing. She died in 1620 at the age of 92, leaving 367 descents, including nine great-great-grandchildren. Lenham Court in Old Ham Lane was once owned by the two 18th century Prime Ministers William Pitt, father and son.

LINTON

Linton's village sign swings in a sturdy timber frame supported by relatively ornate wrought iron brackets and surmounted by more wrought ironwork that includes the encircled Kent badge. It stands opposite The Bull Inn on Linton Hill and unlike most village signs, this one has its own spotlight.

Inside the rectangle of the sign, a painted shield is quartered with symbols of local significance: a stag, recalling the one-time deer park; the church; a group of oast kilns; and a cricket wicket with a bat and ball. The name of the village is in bold lettering on a plain label across the centre.

Nearby St Nicholas' Church contains monuments to former owners of Linton Park, including Sir Horace Mann, whose grandfather built the mansion that Horace Walpole, the 18th century writer, described as "that citadel of Kent, with the Weald as its garden".

There are also monuments to 17th century Sir Anthony Mayne and his wife, Lady Brigett, and to members of the Cornwallis family. The first Lord Cornwallis, who died in 1936, was known as The Squire of Kent and his successor, who was born at Linton in 1892, was a formidable Kent cricketer and was Lord Lieutenant of Kent from 1944 until 1972.

A rather less happily distinguished local inhabitant was that Thomas Hardyng, a mason, who had his head spiked on the gateway to the Palace of Westminster for his part in the conspiracy to force Richard II to keep promises made to Wat Tyler's rebels on Blackheath in 1381.

LOOSE

Loose, a near neighbour of Maidstone, has two village signs: one in the village centre, by the church, and another at Linton crossroads.

The design is an adaptation of a competition winning entry by a Cornwallis School pupil and it was originally a painted sheet metal sign made at the Medway College of Art and Design. But time and the weather did not treat that one well and in 1974 the present cast alloy sign was made by Bernard Hill, of Coxheath, using the same design but this time in painted relief.

The sign is boxed in an oak frame, with the name of the village in bold white lettering across the top of it. For the rest, four round medallions, wreathed in trailing hop bine, illustrate local features: the village church of All Saints; one of the 13 water mills once driven by the stream that runs through the village; the Kent White Horse with a chequered shield that symbolises The Chequers public house; and a brown trout such as once flourished in the stream.

One explanation for the village name is that it derives from Old English for pigsty, and that the village grew up around a Saxon pig farm. Another suggests it describes the way the stream loses itself underground from time to time on its way to join the Medway at Tovil.

But the early prosperity of Loose derived from the Kentish woollen industry when the local water mills were used in the fulling process that removed natural oils from the fleeces.

LUDDESDOWN

It is often a surprise to come across a sign worthy of a much more high profile village in some back of beyond little community with very little to say for itself. The sign at Luddesdown is one of those.

It is a quite imposing piece of ironwork: an arch-topped rectangle with the village name across the bottom in bold, gold-coloured lettering. Within the frame, horizontal and vertical divisions separate silhouettes of a sheaf of corn and the church from a lower tableau of a man and a horse ploughing. The whole is topped by a head-high pheasant.

There is no recognizeable village of Luddesdown, which consists of a remotely rural Downland community south of Cobham, which is itself south of Gravesend. It is of respectable antiquity, however. Luddesdown Court, near the church, is credited with being one of the oldest inhabited houses in England, perhaps dating from around 1100, but evidence of early Iron Age and even Stone Age occupation has been found nearby. The 13th century church of SS Peter and Paul was largely rebuilt in 1866 but the tower has Roman tiles built into it.

A mile or two south of Luddesdown Dode Church is all that remains of a village that was virtually wiped out by the Black Death in 1349, after which the church fell into disuse and serious disrepair. But it was restored in 1905 and is now privately owned.

LYMINGE

Lyminge is a large village eight or nine miles inland from Folkestone, in the beautiful Elham Valley. The oldest part is just off the B2065 which snakes through it southward to Hythe and here the church remains as a memorial to the abbey that was founded in 633 by Ethelburga, daughter of King Ethelbert, the first Christian King of Kent. She was married to Edwin of Northumbria and it was after he died that she returned to Kent and founded the kingdom's first nunnery, of which she became abbess. The associated monastery was the earliest in England after St Augustine arrived here in 597.

She it is who is pictured on the village sign as a blue-gowned shepherdess, turning her back on the steam engine which looks as though it is emerging from the church behind it. It serves as a reminder of the old Elham Valley Railway, which opened in 1899 and was responsible for encouraging the development of Lyminge into a small market town. The line was closed in 1947, however, and became a popular public walk, while the little railway station became the local branch of the public library.

The wooden sign has the name of the village carved into it and the wavy lines beneath that refer to the Nailbourne stream which flows - once every seven years, according to local lore - through the valley.

LYNSTED

It is always a particular pleasure to discover something unusual and the attractive North Kent village of Lynsted, south of Teynham, has one of the most unusual of all village signs in Kent.

It is in the form of a disc mounted on the sloping top of a concrete "tree trunk" at the end of a paved area leading to it on the other side of the road from the Black Lion public house.

The sign itself acknowledges that it was made by children of the parish and by artist Amanda Randall in 1996 and the design is packed with local detail in the sort of lively style that only children seem able to achieve.

Named streets of the village thread through illustrations of local houses, the church, an oast house, the pub, the peacock gates of the house called Bogle and the school is represented by a boy and a girl at play in the centre. The antiquity of the village is illustrated with a group of Roman soldiers, a coach and horses and a lorry; there is an aeroplane to remind us that this was Battle of Britain country and representations of fruit and hops bear witness to the agricultural character of the neighbourhood.

Nearer the roadside, in front of the sign, is a colourful display board showing the public rights of way around Lynsted, put there "in celebration of the Golden Jubilee of Queen Elizabeth II, 2002."

The involvement of the school children in creating the sign bodes well for the future of the village, when the children will take pride in "their" village sign and be able to point out their contribution to their own children.

MARDEN

This smartly timber-framed sign stands in the middle of Marden, to one side of the High Street. It features the village stocks outside the church door, flanked by a crowned village pump and a fruit tree, with a garland of hops on the bine across the top. The name of the village is in bold red letters across the bottom and the whole is surmounted by a wrought iron shield containing the White Horse badge of Kent.

The old court house, where the stocks originally were, still stands in the village as a reminder that this was once part of the Royal manor of Milton Regis and, as a Royal Hundred, was exempt from the jurisdiction of the county sheriff. Marden began life as one of those "dens" in The Weald which North Kent manors annexed as woodland pastures in which to fatten their pigs. Later, it shared in the prosperity of the Wealden woollen industry and, later still, was part of the Kentish fruit and hops farming region.

One of the treasures of the Church of St Michael and All Angels at Marden is the stained glass in the chancel, which was designed by Patrick Reyntiens in 1952 to represent the vision of St John described in Revelations.

MATFIELD

The distinction between the closely neighbouring villages of Brenchley and Matfield is blurred these days. Recent building has virtually run the two into one and if Matfield did not have its own village sign, visitors unfamiliar with the local geography might not even realise it was distinct from its neighbour.

The characters of the two are, however, very different, and so are the signs that identify them.. The Matfield sign, which stands on the village green takes the form of a wrought iron hoop with the word Matfield spelled out in wrought iron letters across the middle. Above the name, two apples dangle from the top of the hoop and there are cherries underneath framing the date, 1981, in a diamond-shaped frame.

The fruit acknowledges the orchards that, once to a greater extent than today, characterised this part of the Weald, which was a major part of the famous Blossom Tours route in springtime, when coachloads of tourists navigated the local roads in order to marvel at the tinted clouds of blossom in the roadside orchards.

Unlike most Kent villages, Matfield has a relatively modern Victorian sandstone church, built in the last quarter of the 19th century. The First World War poet Siegfried Sassoon was born in Matfield, but is buried elsewhere, although his brother, Hamo, is remembered on the war memorial.

While the Battle of Britain was fought overhead in 1940, Matfield found itself in the news because of the double murder of Dorothy Fisher and her housemaid Charlotte Saunders, for which Dorothy's husband's lady-friend, widowed Florence Ransome, was convicted and sent to Broadmoor.

MEOPHAM

Meopham (pronounced Meppum, by the way) Historical Society donated this sign, which was made of steel by local craftsmen, to the village to commemorate its 25th anniversary in July 1998, and the notice fixed to the upright permits of no ambiguity about that.

This is one of those "cut-out" signs, on which the symbols themselves form the outline with no frame. The name of the village, in black-on-white lettering, makes a platform on which stand two prominent landmarks, the church (St John the Baptist) and the early 19th century smock mill. Below the name is a cricket wicket, bat and ball, a reference to the long connection of the game with the village, where it has been played on the village green, next to the windmill, since 1746. The upright itself is capped with a bishop's mitre.

Meopham, almost due south of Gravesend on the A227, takes some pride in being the longest village in Kent. It was here, in the 14th century church of St John the Baptist, that John Tradescant, Charles I's Dutch gardener, was married in 1607 and his son, also John, was christened there a year later. They were both botanists and introduced many plants that have become favourites with gardeners although they were hitherto unknown in this country.

MEREWORTH

One of several "millennium" village signs is the one at Mereworth which is a colourful pictorial sign, featuring the unique Palladian-style church of St Lawrence, which was built in the first half of the 18th century and modelled on an Inigo Jones church in Covent Garden, London. The spire, which is probably the most incongruous village church spire in Kent, was copied from that of St Martin in the Field, also in London.

On the sign, the church is surrounded by hops, soft fruit and other rural symbolism, with scattered gravestones, one of which is inscribed "1999 RIP". The name of the village is in black on white across the bottom.

A plaque on the upright timber, which is planted in a small area of grass beside the A228 near its junction with the A26 Maidstone-Tonbridge road, tells passers-by that the sign was designed by Hannah Adamaszek, a local artist, to celebrate the 2000 AD Millennium.

The present village of Mereworth did not grow up where it is but was moved from its original pre-Saxon site, a quarter of a mile away, by the 18th century builder of so-called Mereworth Castle because it spoiled his view from his new home. He was the Hon John Fane, who later inherited the title of Earl of Westmorland.

MILSTEAD

The name Milstead describes a "milk place", probably a small dairy farm providing milk for a surrounding area, and the village sign illustrates this with a milkmaid carrying pails of milk hung from a yoke across her shoulders.

The carved wooden sign stands on the little patch of green at the road junction just outside the village hall where its companion is a handsome conifer tree with a wooden seat all round it, which is also featured on the sign.

The name of the village is carved across the bottom and the domed wooden frame is carved symetrically with, starting from the bottom, cricket wickets with balls, cherries, horse-shoes, apples, pears and more cherries at the top. The whole sign is supported on scrolled metal brackets springing from a timber upright.

Milstead is a very small cross-roads village on the Downs south of Sittingbourne and, more immediately, just south of the M2. The village church of St Mary and the Holy Cross stands above the road that passes it: a mainly Early English and Perpendicular building with earlier, possibly Saxon but much restored, remnants.

In the churchyard is a stone slab which covers the access to the Tylden family vault and inside the church is a Tylden Chapel where lie several members of the same family. The Tyldens lived in the Tudor manor house opposite the church.

MINSTER-IN-THANET

The "in-Thanet" is necessary to distinguish this village from the Minster on the Isle of Sheppey. Both took their names from very early religious houses, this one established, as the village sign proclaims, in AD 670.

The name of the village follows the domed top of the sign, which depicts a white deer flanked by woodland trees, illustrative of the legend of how the parish was founded. That relates that King Egbert of Kent agreed to give to his sister Ermenburga, Queen of Mercia, as much land as would be covered by her pet deer in one day's coursing, in compensation for his murder of her two sons. On the land, the queen founded a minster at which she became the abbess, taking the religious name of Domneva. She was succeeded by her daughter Mildred who died in 725 was canonised in 1388, becoming the patron saint of the Isle of Thanet.

The original convent was completely destroyed by the Danish invasion of 841, and not rebuilt until the 12th century. It was then inhabited by monks from St Augustine's, Canterbury, for more than 500 years before it became a private house during the Reformation and was restored to a religious community by Bavarian refugee Benedictine nuns in 1937. Now it is visited by large numbers of tourists every year.

NEWENDEN

Right on the very edge of Kent, where the River Rother separates the county from East Sussex, Newenden even looks rather like a frontier village. It is little more than St Peter's Church and the White Hart Inn on opposite sides of the A28.

But its village sign, opposite the inn, makes up for everything it lacks in other respects. It is strikingly different from any other Kent sign.

For a start, it is triangular, with the name prominent in gold coloured cut-out lettering across the top. Inside the frame is a composite representation of the four evangelists of the New Testament. The symbolic creature has a lion's head (St Mark), ox's hooves (St Luke), eagle's wings (St John) and a child looking forward into the new millennium on the creature's back (St Mathew). The serpent's tail represents the river which has sustained the village from its earliest days.

Around the border, the pattern represents a maze, with flowing lines to describe the river, and in the top two corners, cricket balls refer to the village's claim that the first recorded game of cricket was played in Newenden, 700 years ago. At the foot of the triangle are the crossed keys of St Peter.

All this symbolism reflects that on the church font, which is famously finely carved, although variously interpreted.

Until storms changed the course of the River Rother in the mid-13th century, Newenden was a river port of some importance. Romans knew it as Andredscaster, to Saxons it was Eopenburnen and it was the site of one of the earliest Carmelite houses in England.

OFFHAM

To everyone who is familiar with the Mid Kent villages, Offham is "the one with the quintain". The mediaeval equestrian sporting apparatus has long been the single most distinctive feature of the village, on its piece of village green alongside the Teston Road.

But now it is joined by the village sign which stands nearby and of which, inevitably, the quintain is the dominant feature, occupying the top central area of the upright oblong sign and flanked by vertical panels of representative greenery and cherries. A central horizontal label carrying the name of the village separates the quintain from two silhouetted oast kilns between panels containing, on one side, a pear and on the other side an apple.

The sign, on its sturdy timber upright, is framed with fairly exuberant decorative ironwork and the whole thing very much reflects the character of the local countryside in which this picturesque village centre belongs.

St Michael's Church, on a low hill a mile from the village centre, dates from about 1100, after William the Conqueror's Domesday surveyors named Offham as part of the extensive land holdings in Kent of Odo, Bishop of Bayeux, and local quarries provided stone for Roman building work and for cannon balls for the defence of Henry VIII's realm. The 14th century Jack Straw who featured prominently in Wat Tyler's Peasants' Revolt in 1381 may have been born in the parish.

OTHAM

The Mid Kent village of Otham is distinguished with another of those sometimes controversially different village signs, this one having been chosen by villagers' ballot in 1997.

That was when the restored sign was returned to its original site on the village green, a near neighbour of the war memorial and not far from St Nicholas' Church.

But so unusual is it that some villagers felt the need for restoration offered an opportunity to scrap it altogether and replace it with something less unconventional, and others, while they didn't mind the design, thought its siting was inappropriate.

However, a referendum organised by the parish council determined that it should remain where it was and so it did.

The sign is, in fact, a skeletal metal box containing, as the plaque on the ragstone plinth into which the steel upright is set puts it: "The tools that shaped our village."

From the top of its supporting upright, the stainless steel "tool-box" looks across the green to an impressive view of part of The Weald, on the southern edge of Maidstone.

The River Len flows towards the Medway at Maidstone past Otham and although the name of the village is most reliably said to derive from the name of the Saxon family that founded it (or, perhaps, "acquired" it from earlier inhabitants), it has been suggested that the name might, instead, indicate a former abundance of otters hereabouts. With place-names, it is often a matter of picking the derivation that most takes your fancy.

PLATT

The village sign at Platt, just off the A25 south-west of Borough Green, stands like an inverted exclamation mark beside the church, as though the parish were announcing its identity in spite of the fact that it is completely overlooked by most of the county literature.

The metal sign sits on the top of its timber upright on a raised piece of walled green next to the church, opposite Long Mill Lane. The sign itself is in the form of a disc displaying an arrangement of hops and cob nuts, within a double metal frame. Over the top, the sign identifies itself with the words PLATT PARISH and at the bottom the date, AD 2000. This is another of those village signs that were erected to mark the millennium.

Platt is another of Kent's hideaway communities. It does not compel travellers to find it en route to somewhere else, nor encourage them to seek it out for any special feature or features although some of the 18th century domestic architecture is distinctive enough to earn a mention in reference books. It is a very compact little village gathered around its stone-built St Mary's Church, from which it takes the name of St Mary's Platt to distinguish it from other Kent villages with similar names. Although architecturally of Early English design, the church was actually built in 1841-2, at a cost of less than £3,500.

PLAXTOL

The head of the Roman goddess Minerva is the village sign at Plaxtol, at the top of a tall timber upright that stands on the little triangle of green known as Plaxtol Spoute, recalling the discovery of a statuette when a Roman villa was excavated on the banks of the river Bourne in 1857. There was a Roman cemetery, too, at nearby Ducks Farm.

The Romans revered Minerva, daughter of Jupiter, as one of their principal deities, and they made her patroness of all the arts and handicrafts, as well as being their goddess of war.

In fact, Plaxtol could be said to have two village signs because, as well as the Minerva, outside the church wall is a new Millennium stone with an inset plaque recording that the village population in AD 2000 was 1,051, that there were 402 dwellings and that it covered 972 hectares.

Old Soar Manor house, now owned by the National Trust, is in Plaxtol and there are several other old houses in the parish. But the church is unique in Kent, having been built during the Cromwellian Commonwealth and, because of that, having no dedication. Until Victorian restorers had their way with it, it was the only complete 17th century church in Kent but it was substantially altered in the last quarter of the 19th century.

PLUCKLEY

This, of course, is the reputed most haunted village in England, but there is no reference to that on the village sign, which contents itself with a very restrained painted rural scene featuring the steepled church in the foreground and a round-kiln oast house farther back. The name of the village is prominent in gold-coloured letters across the bottom.

The shape of the sign, however, does reflect the other thing for which Pluckley is noted: the so-called Dering windows that are a feature of many local buildings. They are said to be the result of the discovery by a member of the once prominent Dering family that one of his forebears escaped the consequences of backing the wrong side during the Civil War through such a window. As a result, the 19th century Sir Edward Cholmeley Dering had all the windows on his estate replaced with windows with domed tops, sometimes described as looking as though they were raising their eyebrows upon the local scene.

The village lies to the west of Ashford, south of Charing, on the B2077, its centre dominated by St Nicholas' Church and the Black Horse public house. A black horse featured on the Dering family arms, but more recently it was the Larking family that brought distinction to the village with the filming there of the television adaptation of H E Bates' The Darling Buds of May.

RUCKINGE

Ruckinge overlooks the Royal Military Canal from the old shoreline above Romney Marsh and this very distinctive sign is as much a memorial to a former resident as it is an identification of the village. It identifies itself as a facsimile of an Aveling and Porter steam road roller smoke box door and it was installed outside Ruckinge village hall in Festival of Britain year, 1951. As well as the name of the village, it has the Kentish White Horse and Invicta motto that featured on the old steam road rollers and a reminder that "Thomas Aveling once farmed at Court Lodge in this parish". The facsimile was presented to the village by Aveling-Barford Ltd.

That much is explained by the sign itself but it is interesting to discover that Thomas Aveling started repairing agricultural machinery in the 1850s and soon began to experiment with steam cultivation. The steam plough he produced in 1856 was so successful that Kent farmers presented him with a 300 guineas (£315) award. In 1858 he opened Invicta Works in Strood, where he produced a variety of agricultural steam engines and after 1867, and well into the 20th century, Invicta steam road rollers were familiar throughout Kent and England, and many were exported to other parts of the world. By 1872, Invicta Works employed 400 men and was the largest makers of steam rollers in the world.

Today, the Strood riverside site is occupied by Medway's Civic Centre but one of the old buildings remains as a memorial to Thomas Aveling and his Invicta Works, one of the largest engineering works in Kent.

SANDHURST

The wrought iron decorative work that surrounds the Sandhurst village sign is almost more eye-catching than the sign itself, which hangs in its rectangular iron frame on a piece of green where Back Road leaves the A268, between Hawkhurst and Newenden.

The dominant feature of the sign is the brick-built clock tower that was built in 1889 by parishioners and friends in memory of Arthur Oakes, JP of Downgate. It is pictured in front of a row of woodland trees and wreathed in a hop bine, a reference to the character of the surrounding countryside and also to the importance of hop growing here, as throughout so much of Kent, during the 19th and the first half of the 20th centuries. The picture is underlined with the name of the village in bold black lettering on a white ground.

The clock tower itself is to be found behind the war memorial in Bodiam Road, a little way to the west of where the village sign is.

Only the most conscientious county guide books give Sandhurst so much as a mention, but the church (St Nicholas), has an impressive 15th century tower once used as a watch tower for nearby Bodiam castle. It stands a mile outside today's village, where it was left when villagers moved to what was regarded as healthier higher land to escape the 14th century Black Death, and part of the churchyard is reputed to contain a plague pit where victims were buried.

SANDLING

On a small green area just across the road from the Kent Trust for Nature Conservation's Tyland Barn shop and education centre stands the sign that proclaims that this small residential area on Maidstone's northern fringe is, in fact, modern Sandling.

It is a rather handsome round sign, quartered with Downland scenery, a three-kiln oast house and the barn itself, all above a spray of hop-bearing bine and with the name SANDLING in white on a red ribbon over the top. The illustrated part of the sign sits in a metal crescent socketed over the substantial timber upright.

A metal plate on the upright relates that the sign was based on ideas submitted by the pupils of Sandling County Primary School in 1993, and that it commemorates the centenary of Boxley Parish Council, 1895-1995.

Boxley village actually lies almost due east of the site of the sign and between the two lie the remains of Boxley Abbey, one of the "sights" not to be missed by mediaeval tourists travelling the pilgrims' way to Canterbury.

A short distance to the north the Stone Age Little Kit's Coty lies in the jumbled confusion that earned it the name of The Countless Stones, and across the A229 from them is the White Horse Stone, linked by legend to the death of the 5th century Jutish warrior Horsa who, with his brother Hengist, drove the Britons out of Kent. Horsa was killed but Hengist declared himself King of Kent, justifying history's claim that it was here that English nationhood began.

SISSINGHURST

Quite exceptionally, the timber frame of Sissinghurst village sign is ogee-shaped, with a barbed point. The name of the village arches over the black and white "castle" that is the main feature, with dark trees on a green dome behind it, and the county White Horse badge on a red ground forms a roundel over the name. The whole is supported by minimally carved brackets that spring from the timber upright.

The sign stands on the roadside grass verge of the A262, opposite the playing field, roughly half-way between Goudhurst and Biddenden and a plaque on the upright reads: "This sign was erected to mark the Sissinghurst Millennium Festival, 21 October 2000".

This is the village that has become world-famous for the gardens created by the writer Vita Sackville-West after she and her husband Harold Nicolson made their home at Sissinghurst Castle in 1930. The house (now owned by the National Trust) began life as a Tudor mansion house built by Richard Baker, who entertained Queen Elizabeth I there during her Progress through Kent and Sussex in 1573 and was afterwards knighted.

It became a "castle" when it housed French prisoners during the Seven Years' War and it was almost gutted by them. After that, it was Cranbrook parish workhouse for half a century and housed farm workers for another 50 years, before the Nicolsons fell in love with it and restored it to its present appearance.

SMARDEN

The village sign at Smarden blends in so well with its surroundings that it is easy to drive right past it without realising it. That is partly because the village itself is one of Kent's most attractive ones and the eye is easily distracted from the plain carved wooden sign standing outside the village hall beside the main street.

But it is a sign that rewards closer inspection for its detail, which includes the church, St Michael the Archangel's, the largest feature at the top of the dome-topped sign. Below that, sheep and a two-kiln oast house recall that this is one of those Wealden villages that prospered first on wool and, later, on hops and they flank a carving of Queen Elizabeth I riding a horse, a recollection of her Royal Progress through Kent and part of Sussex which brought her to Smarden in 1576. During her stay in the village she granted Letters Patent confirming the grant made by Edward III to Archbishop Simon de Mepham of a five-day fair to be held in the village.

The whole is flanked by carved columns of oak leaves and acorns punctuated with apples below which are a butterfly, a bee and a dragon surmounting the figures 2000.

A plaque explains that the sign was erected on Easter Sunday, April 23, 2000 to commemorate the millennium and was designed by Charles Miller and carved by Frank Pearce, "both of this parish".

The 15th century Thatched House near the church was once the home of Agatha Christie's detective, Miss Marple, in the film The Mirror Crack'd.

SNODLAND

Snodland thinks of itself as a small town rather than as a village and it is sometimes difficult to know into which category a place does fit most comfortably.

But for present purposes, at any rate, its identity badge is a village sign - indeed more than one sign because, village or town, Snodland is not content with just one.

Coming in from the south and leaving the bypass at the roundabout to travel through the village centre, the visitor first encounters a free standing red-and-yellow brick wall with a domed and shouldered top into which is set a white disc on which is the shield-shaped sign over the name, Snodland in black on white lettering.

The sign itself depicts the main local features: a diagramatic cement factory, the local landmark clock tower, and All Saints' Church. The River Medway is represented flowing past all three and a black tree grows out of the river itself.

A few yards further on, Snodland announces itself with a more conventional metal sign that also acknowledges twinship with Moyeuvre-Grand in France and displays the badges of the two towns. Here, the same local features are represented slightly differently.

Human settlement hereabouts can be traced back to before Roman times but its heyday began with the 19th century boom that turned it from a small agricultural community into an industrial centre within a generation, first as a source of bricks for a rapidly expanding London, then as the home of the Charles Townsend Hook paper mills and, more recently, because of the development of the Holborough cement factory.

STAPLEHURST

Staplehurst has had its village sign since 1985, when it was unveiled by the chairman of the National Federation of Women's Institutes.

It stands beside the main road through the village, in a small grassed area in front of the library and to one side of the parking area in front of the shops. It is box-framed in timber and painted with a scene that includes an oast house, the church and a tree-lined road. The name is in bold lettering across the bottom.

The frame is supported on scrolled iron brackets and the timber upright bears a metal plate inscribed: "This sign was commissioned by Staplehurst WI to commemorate Promotion Year 1984. The project was made possible by donations from villagers, tradesmen and local industry."

The plate also names the designer, David Coveney, craftsmen Bernard Hill and Gordon Gracie, and Mrs Anne Harris, who unveiled the sign on May 22, 1985.

The village is probably best-known for its church door, possibly the oldest in England, which is decorated with a few remnants of ironworked pagan symbolism. But there is also, tucked into the roadside hedge, a stone memorial to five local people who were executed for their Protestant convictions during the 16th century reign of Bloody Mary.

It was just outside Staplehurst that Charles Dickens was involved in a serious train crash in June 1865. He never entirely recovered from the experience and, in fact, died exactly five years later, on the anniversary of the crash.

STOCKBURY

Stockbury was an early entry in the record of Kent village signs, with a sign beside the A249 Maidstone-Isle of Sheppey road that featured three squirrels (a reference to the nearby public house of that name), the hilltop church and a harrow (the name of the inn at the village centre).

But the millennium gave the village the incentive to replace the old sign with a new one which has more to say about the history of this very old settlement. It stands on the green in front of The Harrow Inn and has the benefit of a very helpful label on the post which explains all the symbolism.

The "cut-out" sign is topped by a motte and baillie castle, a local feature from 1086 or earlier for which there is now very little evidence, near the church. Beyond the castle palisade a mediaeval ploughman follows his two-oxen plough and below him is the e, and the date 1086. Below that again, a decorative label bears the date 2000 and the modern name, Stockbury, Kent, with the county White Horse badge on a shield under that.

Saxon name of the village, Stochingeberge, and the date 1086. Below that again, a decorative label bears the date 2000 and the modern name, Stockbury, Kent, with the county White Horse badge on a shield under that.

Stockbury's mention in the Domesday Survey of 1086, when it was part of the very extensive lands of Bishop Odo of Bayeux, (the explanation on the sign renders it Bayeur), Norman Earl of Kent, assessed the land in arable cultivation as two sulungs (about 400 acres) and recorded that there was, a church, a mill and woodland, together worth £6.

SUNDRIDGE

The timber upright of the shield-shaped painted sign at Sundridge carries a round plaque which records that it was issued to celebrate nine hundred years of Norman heritage. It reads: "This Community is recorded in the Domesday Book 1086". In the centre of the plaque, the word Domesday has a crown over it and the dates 1086-1986 below it, with the words: "Authorised by the National Domesday Committee".

Below the plaque is another rectangular metal plate which tells us that this village sign, April 1984, was presented by H S M (Peter) Hall Esq (member of Sundridge parish council) (1967-1983), painted by G A Towers Esq, constructed by S F King Esq and erected by G E Rutter Esq.

The sign itself, at the side of the A25 just west of Sevenoaks, is quartered with local scenes on a green ground.

In fact, the village predates the Norman Conquest and the Domesday Survey, having been given to the See of Canterbury by Godwin, Saxon Earl of Kent and father of King Harold. The River Darent flows through Sundridge and the 13th century church, featured on the sign, stands a little apart from the busy village centre on higher ground.

One of the local tourist attractions is nearby Emmetts, five acres of parkland and gardens, now owned by the National Trust, which claims the distinction of being one of the highest gardens in Kent.

SUTTON VALENCE

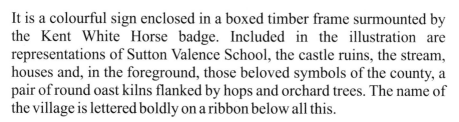

The view across the Weald from the hill on which Sutton Valence stands is spectacular, and some hint of it is to be seen in the village sign, which stands beside the main road through the village (the A274) outside Sutton Valence School.

Another millennium sign, the £2,000 it cost was shared by the parish council and the local branch of the Women's Insitute and it was designed by WI members Grace Case and Audrey Bishop. It was made by Coxheath's Bernard Hill.

It is a colourful sign enclosed in a boxed timber frame surmounted by the Kent White Horse badge. Included in the illustration are representations of Sutton Valence School, the castle ruins, the stream, houses and, in the foreground, those beloved symbols of the county, a pair of round oast kilns flanked by hops and orchard trees. The name of the village is lettered boldly on a ribbon below all this.

St Mary's Church at Sutton Valence has a memorial to William Lambe, who was baptised there and went on to become a Freeman of the City of London Company of Clothworkers in 1568. He built almshouses in the village and in 1576 founded Sutton Valence Free Grammar School for about 20 boys. Today, the school occupies about 100 acres and educates both boys and girls.

The village also remembers that John Willes, who first introduced round-arm bowling to cricket, is buried in the churchyard.

TESTON

Several villages have signs that were sponsored by local Women's Institutes, often to commemorate the Institute's 50th anniversary.

The Teston (locally, Teeson) sign is one of these, an all-metal sign with all the ornamentation displayed across the top of the name of the village. It celebrated Teston WI's 50th anniversary in 1970 and was inspired by the Insitute's own banner.

The main features are the Rev James Ramsay, the anti-slavery campaigner, and his black servant and friend for 22 years, Nestor. Ramsay was Rector of Teston and Nettlestead from 1781 until he died in 1787. Nestor died in 1786 and both men are remembered with plaques outside the church.

A spread cricket wicket, bails flying as a ball hits the middle stump, recalls the famous Alfred Reader cricket ball factory that carried the name of Teston throughout the cricket-playing world for almost 200 years. Between these two features, a double circle encloses a stylised local view that includes the church and Teston's particularly fine 14th century five-arch bridge over the River Medway.

When William Cobbett paused here during one of his Rural Rides in 1820, he recorded that the view from the riverside below Teston was one of the most attractive in Mid Kent. Today, the village is almost wholly residential but its country park is one of the "anchors" for the Maidstone millennium project that is making the county town's riverside one of its most attractive features.

TEYNHAM

The church, a sailing barge, cherries, hops and sheep sum up Teynham's slightly backward-looking self-perception on the village sign that stands atop its metal upright set into a brick plinth in Station Road.

St Mary's Church is still there, certainly, and there are sheep to be found in the surrounding countryside, but hops and cherries, which once abounded, are less in evidence today.

It was at Teynham, or possibly at nearby Conyer, that Richard Harris, fruiterer to King Henry VIII, planted the first commercial orchards of cherries and apples in England, after he learned that the king had developed a taste for the fruit during visits to France. As a result, for some four hundred years this part of Kent was, as William Lambarde put it, "the most dainty piece of all our shire".

Because of the way the village has grown out towards the main A2 road, the church looks as if it has slunk away to brood peacefully on the edge of the Swale-side marshlands, where once there was a neighbouring archbishop's residence.

Teynham used to be a creekside port from which local produce was shipped, by sailing barge, to London and Thames-side Kent and it was also a haven for ships seeking shelter from sudden storms in the estuary. But it spread inland after the railway arrived, until it joined up with the commercial opportunism encouraged by the traffic on the Watling Street (A2) London-Dover route.

TOVIL

Tovil has had its village sign, at the bottom of the two hills that cradle the riverside village, since 1991, when it was officially unveiled by the then Mayor of Maidstone, Cllr Daphne Parvin.

The colourful sign, boxed in timber on a solid timber upright, was designed and made by Bernard Hill of Coxheath and it depicts various local features, most of which are no longer there.

In the top left corner is the spire of St Stephen's Church and, beside it, a cockerel represents the weather-cock that once topped it. The dates 1840/1990 say more about how long the church had stood there when the sign was being designed than how long it was in use because it was declared redundant and closed in 1982.

The label bearing the name of the village slants across the sign, with one end wrapped round the tall chimney of the old paper mill, recalling the industry that characterised the village for more than 300 years. The chimney, and another like it, were demolished in 1984.

Other reminders of the paper-making industry are depicted across the bottom of the sign, beneath the river on which a sailing barge is another reminder of times past, when barges on the River Medway were the main means of transport to and from the mills.

Tucked into the bottom left-hand corner of the sign is a medallion bearing the Kent county White Horse badge and the county motto, Invicta.

TROTTISCLIFFE

Trottiscliffe (pronounced Trosley) straggles a bit up the southern slopes of the North Downs but the village centre nestles cosily below them, giving an air of expecting very little from the Great Beyond.

It is identified by a handsome all-metal square sign at the side of the village main road, with the name displayed in gold-coloured lettering across the bottom. The square is quartered, the top two quarters containing a single cowled oast kiln and three symbolic trees, and the bottom two contain a rather handsome version of the Kent horse and a pheasant above some bushes. The outer square is embellished with decorative iron scroll-work and supported on its relatively slender timber upright by scrolled iron brackets.

Trottiscliffe is one of those villages that seems to have wandered away from its church, which has stood in a farmyard, quite some distance from the village centre, certainly since it earned a mention by the Domesday bureaucrats in the 1080s, since when it has become the depository for various archaeological finds from the nearby Coldrum Stones prehistoric burial site.

Luckily for the villagers, the two local inns, both about 500 years old, are much less remote.

Trosley Park, which takes its name from a former Trosley Towers mansion, was one of Kent's first country parks after the World War Two army training camp there was dismembered to give public access to 120 acres of woodlands, scrub and hillside grassland and to some of the most extensive views south across Kent to be found anywhere in the county.

TUNSTALL

The millennium prompted a number of villages to celebrate the occasion with a village sign, sometimes to replace an earlier one and some for the first time. One of the first-timers was Tunstall, near Sittingbourne, which opted for a very picturesque sign that does full justice to an attractive little village.

Standing at the roadside close to the church, it is prettily painted with a rural scene that includes a twin round-kiln oast, the church of St John the Baptist, and a beamed house, all surrounded by garlanded fruit, flowers and corn, with a group of sheep on one side and a squirrel on the other. A hand grasping an arrow, the badge of Kentish militancy, rises from behind an underlining ribbon inscribed TUNSTALL 2000.

The village was the home of Sir Edward Hales, who is impressively commemorated in the church with an effigy of the noble knight in full armour. The Hales were a distinguished Catholic family whose members played prominent roles in events leading up to and during the Civil Wars.

The house on the bend where the road leaves the village centre on its way to Sittingbourne is still called Hales Place and it was here that leaders of the risings in May 1648 met to plan the opposition to the Puritanical County Committee that led to the military defeat of the Royalists in Kent.

In December 1688, Sir Edward's son was arrested and tried for high treason after being involved in the escape from England of James II. He was later released.

ULCOMBE

The village sign at Ulcombe is another of those that was installed to mark the millennium. The brass plate on the timber upright says so, giving the date as 1.1.2000 and the designer as D (Diane) Brace.

There is a bright cheerfulness about the sign itself which is framed in metal with a design that is separated into six parts. The upper two squares depict the church and the sweeping view over the Weald that can be seen from the churchyard. Beneath them are two rectangles, one with a picture of cattle and sheep and the other with a single tree. Imposed on all four is a gold-coloured lozenge with a picture of a perched owl, a reference to the fact that the village lies in what is known locally as the valley of the owls. Across the bottom, on a bright yellow label, the name of the village is written in bold, black lettering.

The design was chosen after the parish council invited ideas when the project was first mooted.

Although altered, enlarged and renovated a number of times down the centuries, All Saints Church at Ulcombe is of Norman origins and is renowned for the Wealden view from its elevated situation above the village. The churchyard contains a yew tree that is said to be the largest and is certainly one of the oldest in Kent, and inside there are several memorials, including the North Chapel, to members of the St Leger family.

UPCHURCH

Inevitably, perhaps, the village sign at Upchurch features the village church of St Mary the Virgin which is the most memorably distinguishing feature of this otherwise fairly modest little village on the inland fringes of the Medway estuary marshland between Sittingbourne and Rainham.

The sign stands on the corner of Horsham Lane, opposite the old infants' school and close to the church: a colourful composition that includes examples of the pottery that was once a feature of the local economy and a sailing barge, garlanded with various fruits and foliage, with the name of the village on a ribbon at the bottom. It is framed in iron, topped with an iron decoration and supported by simple iron brackets. A nice touch is the basket of flowers half-way up the timber upright.

The church is often described as having a candle-snuffer spire, a good description that has stuck. It is a curious two-tier affair, with an octagonal upper part set down on top of a four-sided pyramid. No doubt there is a good reason for the design which, although unusual, is not unique.

The village would have been known to Sir Francis Drake, whose father, Edmund, was vicar here in 1560. Later, during the 19th century London building boom, sailing barges carried river mud and hillside chalk from Upchurch to the Medway- and Thames-side cement factories and brickworks.

UPPER BUSH

Upper Bush is just half a dozen houses at the end of a cul-de-sac off Bush Road at Cuxton and not at all the sort of place you would expect to have its own village sign.

Yet, there it is: a metal frame separated into four squares containing metal silhouettes of a house, a wheatsheaf, a hand plough and an oast house, reflecting the wholly agricultural character of the community that was, until relatively modern times, larger than neighbouring Cuxton.

The sign is surmounted by a pheasant which sits on a metal label on which the name UPPER BUSH is painted in gold coloured lettering, and it is supported by scrolled metal brackets that spring from the substantial timber upright.

Affixed to the upright is a plaque recording the appreciation of residents for the generosity and support of the Kent Messenger newspaper group which sponsored the production of the sign.

The sign was made at The Forge in Cuxton and is a reminder that the hamlet of Bush (now divided into Upper and Lower Bush) was, until ing the 19th century, a much more substantial community than it is today.

after the railway brought the expansion of Cuxton during the 19th century, a much more substantial community than it is today.

After the Second World War, the hamlet was almost entirely swept away, leaving a few fairly isolated buildings. Cuxton lagged behind this 'little brother' but has now caught up and has its own village sign.

WATERINGBURY

Standing at the junction of Tonbridge Road (A26) with Bow Road (B2015), Wateringbury's village sign is a relatively simple design with two cowled hop kilns and a piece of hop bine above the name of the village and a representation of the River Medway below it. The kiln cowls and some of the hop leaves project beyond the circular metal frame which is supported on its timber upright with scrolled wrought iron brackets.

A plaque on the upright tells anyone who cares to read it that the sign was presented by Wateringbury WI to mark the occasion of their 60th anniversary in November 1980.

For many years, the Whitbread Phoenix brewery was a major distinguishing feature of this part of the village but the brewery closed in 1982 and the last part of it, a 100ft high chimney, came down in October 1984. The great golden phoenix weather-vane that identified the brewery and was a distinctive local landmark, survived for a time atop the new hotel that was built near the site, but it was then replaced by a smaller version. In the 18th century brick earth was dug from the woods at the north end of the parish and bricks were made in a kiln built on the common.

Today, most of what industry there is clusters at the riverside and the village is familiar to all River Medway boat users.

WEST MALLING

West Malling thinks of itself as a small town rather than as a village but, even so, it seems a trifle excessive to have no fewer than three different village signs, even if two of them are on the two sides of one sign.

The double sided sign was erected in 1984 on the vestigial village green at the entrance to the village from the A20, where Town Hill merges with High Street. Carved from a single piece of oak, one side is painted with the figure of Gundulph, 11th century Bishop of Rochester, holding tools that symbolise his renown as a builder. Behind him are St Leonard's Tower, a local landmark which he built, and Malling church, and a World War II Spitfire fighter plane dips its wing overhead in memory of the famous airfield, now redeveloped, just outside the village.

The other side shows a game of cricket in progress, with oast houses in the background, a reminder of West Malling's claim to be one of the earliest venues for Kent cricket.

The oak sign has not weathered well and a new sign now stands at the other end of the village, where St Leonard's Street joins Teston Road. It is smaller, single-sided, and it features St Leonard's Tower, a Roman soldier and two Spitfires. Below the bold lettering of the name, two swans, back to back, represent Manor Park Country Park, opposite St Leonard's Tower.

WESTBERE

This picturesque little village off the A28 Canterbury-Thanet road is identified by a sign created from a somewhat complex arrangement of geometric shapes, the outline of which mimics that of the church, All Saints. At the top, a hexagon frames three bells, like the three bells in the open bell-cote of the church. Below them, wavy lines represent the adjacent Westbere Lakes, with a swan and representations of the local flora, and the name of the village is on a label near the bottom of the sign.

A notice on the upright explains that the sign was erected on July 7, 1991 by the parish council to celebrate the gift of land for a village green by John and Christine Stevens of Westbere House and there follows a list of names of people involved in designing and making the sign.

The enclosed village green is opposite the church, and there is also a graveyard which has been designated a wildlife conservation area in which a survey in 1994 identified more than 60 different species of trees, flowers and grasses and many different insects and other wildlife.

It has been claimed that beer took its name from the village because this was where the first hops to be cultivated commercially in Britain were grown, at Hopland Manor, during the 15th century, but it is one of those claims that deserves to be savoured with the proverbial pinch of salt.

WHITFIELD

Whitfield has grown up at the point where two roads part company, one (A2) to loop eastwards down to Dover docks and the other (A256) to drop more directly down the steep incline into Dover town and it is at the roadside near the juction that the village sign is to be found.

The sign itself is a relatively simple one, showing the old church, with the name of the village in gold lettering under it. But it is still unlike any other village sign in Kent for the doll-like masks fixed to the quite slender supporting post. These represent the five sons and six daughters of parishioners William and Jane Cross who died, most of them only a few days old, between November 1821 and August 1835. Only one daughter, Marian, survived to maturity, and even she died before her parents did, in 1860, aged 26.

Whitfield claims to be one of Kent's oldest parishes and there was a church here early in the 11th century which was named St Peter's in about 1070. Two of the original Saxon windows survive.

In 1302-3, a holder of part of the manor did so "by service of holding the king's head between Dover and Wissant whenever he travelled between the two" - evidently the king, Edward I, was not a good cross-Channel traveller.

WITTERSHAM

In the long-ago, before Romney Marsh was drained, the Isle of Oxney rose from the surrounding sea, a true island. Today, it is an area of higher ground amid some of the best farmland in England and Wittersham is its largest village, mid-way between Tenterden and Rye and within a mile or so of the Kent-East Sussex border.

The village sign is small, but with quite elaborately ornate wrought iron scrolled and garlanded supports for the plain black metal sign on which is written: Wittersham Isle of Oxney. The very simple sign is crowned with a rather splendid silhouette of a Roman - or is it Saxon? - galley under full sail.

Although the whole area is today generally included under the label of Romney Marsh, in fact the Isle of Oxney actually overlooks Walland Marsh, the westerly area that overlaps into East Sussex. The River Rother changed its course more than once as a result of storms and flooding, changing the fortunes for better or worse of a number of villages. Wittersham was a winner because the diversion of the river from the north side to the south side of the Isle of Oxney made the village into a river port.

The village church of St John the Baptist has some interesting features and the churchyard contains a number of early 18th century headstones. The tower, a prominent landmark for miles around, once guided ships into the port at night by the light of a beacon on its top.

WORTH

The sign that alerts travellers along the A258 Sandwich-Deal road to the village's existence is very reminiscent of a certain kind of seaside postcard and it beams a welcome to anyone who cares to follow the minor road down to the village itself.

It pictures a local veteran leaning on his walking stick in front of a five-bar field gate and pointing helpfully towards the village, as though giving directions to some visitor uncertain of his whereabouts. Below him is the message: 'There's Good Worth in Word", which is still a bit puzzling even after you are told that the village takes its name from the Old English "word", which meant an enclosure.

The village itself puts a semi-colon rather than a full stop to the road that meanders into and through it, petering out at Worth Creek where, it is said, Archbishop Thomas Becket embarked secretly when he fled England in order to escape the consequences of his dispute with Henry II, and also where Henry V, returning from his St Crispin's Day victory at Agincourt, landed. Local legend claims the king (or, maybe, one of his company) fell in love with a village ale-wife with whom he lived for a time, prompting Worth to give the name of The St Crispin to its village inn.

WROTHAM

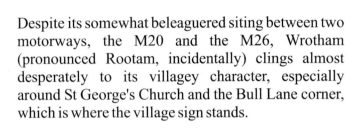

Despite its somewhat beleaguered siting between two motorways, the M20 and the M26, Wrotham (pronounced Rootam, incidentally) clings almost desperately to its villagey character, especially around St George's Church and the Bull Lane corner, which is where the village sign stands.

The sign displays a quartered shield inside a black ironwork frame, across the bottom of which the name of the village stands out in iron lettering. The square frame is topped with the Kent Horse and each top corner is filled with a hop leaf, separated by two bells. The shield is supported on both sides by an ironwork arrangement of fruit, corn and hops and below it a cow and a pig face each other.

The colourful shield is quartered by the red cross of St George and bears, in the top two quarters, a pair of cowled oast kilns and the village church, and beneath them is a earthenware pot inscribed '2000 Wrot" and a pilgrim on a horse, a reference to the fact that Wrotham was on the old pilgrims' route out of London to Canterbury.

A brass plate on the timber upright recalls that the sign, based on an original design by Jim Maloney, was provided by Wrotham Parish Council in partnership with Lawrie Plantation Services Ltd, and was unveiled on April 23, 2000 by Cllr John S Walton.

YALDING

The village sign at Yalding is unusual for being on a bracket fixed to a building, rather than free-standing on a timber upright, as most are.

The main feature of the design painted on the sign is the three-arched bridge, representative of the two fine medieval bridges that cross three rivers at Yalding: the River Medway and its two major tributaries, the Beult and the Tiese. Below the bridge, a conical, cowled oast kiln is flanked on the left by a roundel bearing the key and pen emblems of SS Peter and Paul, to whom Yalding church is dedicated, and on the right another roundel contains a sprig of hops, illustrative of the major role of Yalding in the hop growing industry that was a distinctive feature of Wealden agriculture for some three hundred years.

Yalding's Town Bridge, which crosses the River Beult, was the scene of a Civil War battle in 1643 when Royalist forces surrendered to the Parliamentarians and some of them were held, for a time, in the church.

During the 18th century canal-building boom, the Medway Navigation Company was formed and was responsible for the New Cut across the big bend in the river between Hampstead and Twyford, creating a wharf where barges unloaded coal and took on timber and Wealden iron products. Nothing ever came of plans for a canal joining the River Medway at Yalding with the River Rother at Tenterden and when the railway linked Paddock Wood and Maidstone, the line carried thousands of London hop-pickers to the many hop farms around Yalding.

INDEX